# PURIM

# PURIM

by HOWARD GREENFELD
illustrated by ELAINE GROVE

Holt, Rinehart and Winston · New York

Printed in the United States of America
1    3    5    7    9    10    8    6    4    2

*Library of Congress Cataloging in Publication Data*
Greenfeld, Howard.
Purim.
Summary: Describes the customs associated with
the feast of Purim which celebrates Queen Esther's
victory over the wicked Haman.
1. Purim—Juvenile literature. [1. Purim]
I. Grove, Elaine, ill. II. Title.
BM695.P8G68        296.4'36        82-3058
ISBN 0-03-061478-3            AACR2

ISBN 0-03-061478-3

# PURIM

Purim, the happiest of all Jewish holidays, is celebrated each year on the fourteenth day of the Hebrew month of Adar, which falls in February or March of our calendar. It commemorates the victory of the beautiful and courageous Queen Esther and her wise and good cousin, Mordecai, over Haman, an arrogant tyrant who plotted to destroy the Jewish people many centuries ago.

The name Purim is derived from the Hebrew word *pur*, which means lots—for Haman chose the date for the extermination of the Jews by casting lots. The tyrant failed, and this celebration of his defeat serves as a reminder that all tyrannies may be overcome and that good can always triumph over evil. In the centuries since the defeat of Haman, others have tried to destroy the Jewish people by persecution and murder, but none have succeeded. The festival of Purim is not merely the celebration of a glorious and unexpected victory in the past, but also a call for hope and courage in the future. Its story serves as a vivid demonstration of the ugliness and the ultimate futility of any attempt to eliminate a noble people.

The origins of the holiday of Purim are found in the Book of Esther, one of the most beautiful and moving portions of the Bible. The story is set in the vast Persian Empire during the fourth century B.C.E. (Before the Common Era).

This great kingdom was ruled by King Ahasuerus, a luxury-loving man who often neglected the serious work of governing his empire. He allowed his advisers to make most important decisions, and spent his days eating and drinking.

A generous if negligent ruler, Ahasuerus decided to celebrate the third anniversary of his reign by giving a series of lavish banquets. He invited the officers of his kingdom as well as the common people of Shushan, the capital city of the Persian Empire. At the last of these banquets, the climax of several days of drinking and feasting, the king sent for his wife, Queen Vashti, so that he could show his guests how extraordinarily beautiful she was. To his astonishment, the queen refused to obey his command. Ahasuerus was enraged by this unpardonable defiance of his wishes. He called together his advisers. They convinced him that if he allowed her to go unpunished, he would be setting an example for other wives

throughout the kingdom, who would believe that they, too, could disobey their husbands. In spite of the affection the king felt for Vashti, he dismissed her as his wife and banished her from the palace forever.

Soon afterward, the search for a new queen began. The most beautiful and worthy maidens of the kingdom were summoned to the royal palace to appear before the king, so that he could choose one among them to succeed the disgraced Vashti. For many months they competed for his approval. Finally he made his choice, selecting a beautiful young Jew named Esther. Esther, whose Hebrew name

was Hadassah, had been brought to the court by her guardian and cousin, Mordecai. Even though he knew that there were many Jews in the Persian Empire, Mordecai advised Esther not to reveal her true origins to the king. He feared that anti-Semitism, an ever-present danger, might be directed against his innocent young ward.

To keep an eye on young Esther, Mordecai sought an appointment as a judge, something that was easily arranged by Esther when she became queen. As a judge, he could spend his days at the king's gate, near the royal palace. It was a wise deci-

sion. It enabled him not only to look after his cousin, but also, by chance, to save the life of the king himself. One day while performing his duties, Mordecai overheard two of the royal courtiers plotting the assassination of Ahasuerus. He immediately conveyed the news to Esther, who informed the king of the threat to his life. After an investigation bore out the truth of these charges, the traitors were caught and executed. The queen told her husband of Mordecai's heroism, but the incident, after having been written down in the royal diaries, was quickly forgotten by the absentminded monarch.

Shortly after the revelation of this plot against his life, Ahasuerus appointed a strong and ruthless man, Haman, to the position of chief minister. The arrogant Haman was determined to rule with an iron hand. He would permit no disobedience by any of the king's subjects. To show his confidence in the new chief minister, the king commanded that all who passed before Haman should bow down. The order was obeyed by all, with one exception. In spite of all efforts to make him do so, Mordecai refused to show this sign of respect to a man like Haman. This was because the chief minister was de-

scended from the Amalekites, a people who had long been the enemies of the Jews. Haman was furious at this defiance of his power—so much so that he decided to take his revenge not only on Mordecai but on all Jews who lived in the Persian Empire. He went before the king and invented lies about the Jews. He said that they were different from other peoples of the kingdom and that they were disloyal and refused to obey the king's laws. Ahasuerus, who blindly trusted his chief minister, believed this slander and granted Haman permission to massacre all of the Jewish people on a day to be chosen by Haman. The chief minister was delighted with what seemed to be an easy victory over the Jews. Lots were cast, and it was determined that on the thirteenth day of Adar every Jew in the Persian Empire—young and old, man, woman, and child—would be slaughtered.

Haman looked forward to the date, certain that his hated enemies would be defeated. However, he was unaware of the strength and courage of these people, nor did he know that the queen herself was one of them.

Isolated in her palace, Esther first learned of the cruel decree from her cousin Mor-

decai. Grief stricken, he sent a messenger to tell her of the desperate plight of their people. He begged her to go to the king and plead with him to save their lives—her own included. Only she, as the queen, might convince him of the cruelty of Haman's plot.

Esther was terrified. She replied that neither she nor any man or woman of any rank was permitted to approach the king without having first been summoned. To do so meant certain death, unless—and this rarely happened—the king granted a reprieve by extending the protection of his golden scepter. She told Mordecai that she had not been called before the king for thirty days. This meant that a summons would soon come, and that it was best to await that time before entering her plea. But Mordecai disagreed, and he sent her more messages, insisting that there was no time to lose and warning her that even she, the queen, would be a victim of Haman's plot.

Finally, Esther realized that she had to act quickly to save the lives of her people. She asked Mordecai to assemble the Jews of Shushan and tell them to observe three days of fasting. She would do the same in order to gather the courage to face the

king. Recognizing her duty, she concluded bravely, as the Bible tells us: "If I perish, I perish."

For three days, Esther and the other Jews of Shushan fasted, after which the queen went to Ahasuerus. She approached his throne cautiously, fearing the consequences of her bold act. When the king saw her, he was overcome by her beauty and her goodness and extended his golden scepter to her, thereby granting her a reprieve from the law that would have called for her execution. He asked what he could do for her, promising to grant any wish she might make, even if it was a request for half his kingdom. Esther, relieved by the kindness of the king's reception, nonetheless sensed that it was not yet the time to ask for the salvation of her people. Instead, she replied that she had come to invite him, together with Haman, to take part in a banquet she had prepared. The king eagerly agreed, and at once ordered his chief minister to join him at the feast.

During the splendid feast, the king again asked what he could do for Esther, and again offered her half his kingdom if it would please her. Feeling once more that it was not yet time to make her request,

Esther asked that the king and Haman join her at a second banquet, during which she would make her petition.

Haman left the feast in high spirits. He was honored to have been included in the first banquet and even prouder to be invited to the second. His joy was diminished only by the fact that Mordecai, who passed him as he left the palace, again refused to bow down before him. Once home, he told his wife and friends of the lavish feast and of the honors that had been bestowed upon him. But he complained bitterly that all this meant little to him as long as the Jew Mordecai contin-

ued to defy his authority. To calm the arrogant tyrant, his wife and friends urged that he immediately have a gallows built on which to hang Mordecai. Pleased with this suggestion, he ordered that the gallows be erected at once. More than ever certain that his enemy would soon be put to death, Haman would be able to attend the second banquet in a happy frame of mind.

The night before the second banquet, the king was restless. Unable to sleep, he ordered that the royal diary be read to him, as a way of passing the time. As he listened to the chronicle, he was re-

minded that Mordecai had once saved his life, and he was shocked when he realized that no reward had been given to the good man. He called for Haman, who was at that moment entering the palace to demand the immediate execution of the defiant Jew, and asked his chief minister what should be done for a man the king wanted to honor above all others. Haman, certain that he was the one to be honored, suggested that such a noble man be dressed in the robes of royalty, paraded proudly through the streets of the capital and proclaimed a hero by the king's herald. Ahasuerus agreed and, to Haman's dismay, revealed that the man to be honored was Mordecai. To make matters worse for the tyrant, the king commanded Haman to lead the procession, announcing the heroism of the Jew to the people of Shushan.

Haman had no choice but to do as the king commanded. When he returned home after the humiliating procession, he told his wife and friends of his disgrace. They were shaken, and for the first time they expressed doubts that Haman could successfully carry out his plot. As they finished speaking, the king's couriers arrived to take the now wary chief minister to Queen Esther's second banquet.

This banquet was a dramatic one. After the king again asked Esther what he could do for her, the courageous queen spoke out with passion. She told Ahasuerus of the plan to massacre the Jewish people, and she revealed herself to be one of them. She pleaded with him to spare the lives of all the Jews. The king, though he himself had unthinkingly authorized the destruction of Esther and her people, was horrified. He asked Esther to remind him who was responsible for the plot, and the queen pointed to the trembling Haman. Ahasuerus was furious, realizing that he had been deceived by his chief minister. Despite Haman's tearful pleas, the king ordered that his treacherous minister be hung on the same gallows that had been meant for Mordecai.

The Jewish people were saved, and their sadness was transformed into joy. Following the execution of Haman, the king appointed Mordecai chief minister of the empire. Though by law even the king could not revoke the edict calling for the murder of the Jews—a royal edict was irrevocable—he issued a second proclamation commanding that the Jews arm and defend themselves against those who would attempt to slaughter them.

On the thirteenth day of Adar, the Jewish people did as they had been commanded. Emboldened by the king's new decree, they arose and defeated their enemies. After their stunning victory, it was proclaimed that the following day be celebrated each year by feasting and rejoicing, by exchanging gifts of food, and by giving generously to the poor. The annual festival came to be known as Purim, or the Festival of Lots.

Today Purim remains a special holiday. It is free from the solemnity that marks most Jewish holidays and is enjoyed above all by children.

For some Jews it is preceded by a day of fasting, a reminder of the fast of Esther. For most, however, the celebration begins joyfully on the evening before the fourteenth of Adar, with a reading of the Megillah, the scroll containing the Book of Esther. Instead of listening to this reading in silence, the children, who are assembled in the synagogue or at home, twirl gragers (noisemakers), stamp their feet, or boo and hiss each time the name of Haman is mentioned. Any noise that serves to drown out the name of this evil man is permitted.

On the morning of Purim, the Book of

Esther is recited again, and once more the name of the tyrant is greeted by noise-makers and catcalls. The name of this man who tried to destroy the Jewish people must be erased, though the courage of those who defeated him must not be forgotten, especially by the young.

For this reason, children often dress in the costumes of Esther, Mordecai, Ahasuerus, or Haman. They entertain their friends and families by acting out the events of this dramatic story. In some parts of the world, especially in Israel, both children and adults attend parades and carnivals, enjoying colorful processions enlivened by floats and masked figures who sing and dance to celebrate the triumph of good over evil.

On Purim the gratitude of the Jewish people is expressed by the *shalach monos*—the sending of gifts of food to friends and to the less fortunate. All should share in this uniquely happy occasion.

The climax of this long day of celebration takes place at home with the *Purim Seudah*, a huge and lavish family feast. This meal ends with the eating of *Hamantaschen*, small three-cornered pastries filled with prunes or poppy seeds and honey, which represent the three-cornered hat worn by

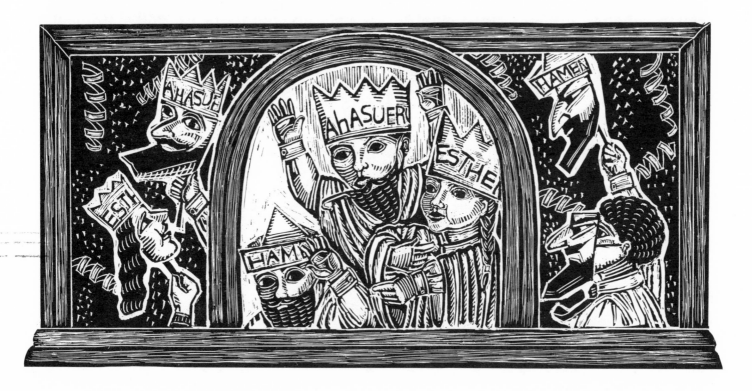

Haman. There is no limit to the number of *Hamantaschen* that may be eaten, just as there is no limit to the joy and merriment of this happiest of Jewish holidays.